COMMENTARIES
elucidating poetics

COMMENTARIES
elucidating poetics

Sutanuka Ghosh Roy

Hawakal
PUBLISHERS
CALCUTTA   NEW DELHI

hawakal

CALCUTTA | NEW DELHI

HAWAKAL PUBLISHERS

33/1/2 K B Sarani, Mall Road, Calcutta 80
70-B/9 Amritpuri, East of Kailash, New Delhi 65

Email info@hawakal.com
Website www.hawakal.com

First edition January, 2021

Cover art: Shutterstock
Cover design: Bitan Chakraborty

ISBN: 978-81-948538-8-6

Price: INR 350 | USD 11.99

For *Baba*

REVIEWS – WHAT AND WHY?

The first question that comes to mind is what is a book review? A book review is a method of literary criticism, they are written opinions about a particular book. They can take many forms. Book reviews can either be brief or long. They can critique and/or abridge the book. They can sometimes be written by readers or professional book reviewers. Reader reviews have a propensity to be more personal, focusing on the individual reader's know-how while reading the book. Since readers can have extensively differing views of the same book, when a book has a variety of reader reviews available, it becomes important for all the stakeholders.

Now let us go back in time twenty years when the internet was a newborn babe. I can recall that I bought books by walking into bookstores, finding a book in a genre I liked that had an interesting cover, read the blurb, and if I deemed the story interesting enough to continue reading, I purchased the book. Reviews were then probably not involved, though friends' recommendations likely were. If I had to choose between two books and a friend had suggested one of them, I would choose the one my friend liked.

Book reviews make books a known quantity. They lessen the risk to readers that a particular book will be not what they had in mind. To put it differently, book reviews help potential readers become familiar with what a book is about, give them an idea of how they might react to it, and decide whether this particular book will be the right book for them at the moment.

Book reviews usually save the time of the readers, in a way make them ready for what they will find, and provide them a better chance of connecting with a certain book, even before they read the first page! Book reviews give books better visibility and a greater chance of getting found by more readers. In today's hectic world, when one looks into different websites, books that have more book reviews are more likely to be shown to potential readers and prospective buyers as compared to books that have few or no reviews. Book reviews also augment the book's reach among book clubs, bookstores, blogging communities, and other opportunities to increase attention from new readers. For an author, book reviews can open doors to new and larger audiences.

Right from our childhood days, we are more or less familiar with the phrase–"Success begets success." Books that have a lot of reviews appear to be popular books. It is human nature to be naturally curious about what looks popular and we want to check it out for ourselves. As a result, a good number of book reviews can help lead to a knock-on effect on book sales.

In other words, the charisma of book reviews can corroborate the worthiness of a book and ascertain who the book's reader is. Once validated, similar people with similar reading tastes are inclined to join their peers and buy that same book.

Sutanuka Ghosh Roy
Kolkata
November 2020

ACKNOWLEDGMENTS

Some of these reviews have been published in *Lapiz Lazuli*, *Setu*, *Life And Legends*, *Muse India*, *Kitaab*, *Fiar*, University of Belfield, Germany. *Kervan, International Journal of Afro-Asiatic Studies, University of Turin*, Italy. *TEXT, Journal of Writing and Writing Courses*, Australia. I'm thankful to the editors of these journals and magazines. It is always a privilege and an honour to review a book, for it broadens the mental horizon. I thank my *Baba*, Professor Baridbaran Ghosh, President, *Bangiya Sahitya Parishad*, Kolkata, for sowing the seed of critical inquiry in me. Ever since my childhood, I have always been inspired by his book reviews. I also thank my teachers for helping me understand the genre. I am also thankful to the academic fraternity, my close friends, and my daughter for their constant support and belief in me.

I thank the author and publisher Bitan Chakraborty and the entire team of Hawakal Publishers for bringing my dream into a reality by publishing my book. I would also like to extend my heartfelt gratitude to poet Dr. Kiriti Sengupta for suggesting the title of the book and also for his constant support, expertise, and care in publishing this book.

CONTENTS

A Resilient Tale: a review of *Sita's Sisters*

Sita's Sisters is the sixth book of poetry by Sanjukta Dasgupta, former professor, head and dean, faculty of Arts, Calcutta University. She is a poet, critic, and translator. She is the recipient of numerous national and international grants and fellowships and has lectured, taught, and read her poems in India, Europe, the USA, and Australia. She is a member of the General Council of Sahitya Akademi New Delhi and Convenor of the English Advisory Board, Sahitya Akademi. Her published books include *Snapshots* (poetry), *Dilemma* (poetry), *First Language* (poetry), *More Light* (poetry), *Her Stories* (translations), *Manimahesh* (translation), *Media, Gender and Popular Culture in India: Tracking Change and Continuity*, *SWADES—Tagore's Patriotic Songs* (translation),

Abuse and Other Short Stories, Lakshmi Unbound (poetry) 2017.

The volume under review is an important collection of poetry in the times we live in. Long ago Helene Cixous in *The Laugh of the Medusa,* wrote, "Woman must put herself into the text – as into the world and into history – by her own movement." Dasgupta in *Sita's Sisters* puts her poetic persona into the text, crafts poetry about resilience and spirit in the face of tragedy, but unlike other poetry in the genre, *Sita's Sisters* does not hammer it in. In the Preamble to *Sita's Sisters* the poet writes, "In selecting *Sita's Sisters* as the title poem of my sixth volume of poetry, I feel the battle for gender equality and gender justice will have to go on, in a resolute and concerted manner, till the battle is won, no matter how long it may take. After all, not unlike a man, a woman can be destroyed but not defeated".

In the first four poems of the collection— "Sita's Sisters," "Sita's lament," "Sita and the Golden Deer," and "Sita Meets Lakshmi," facts are stated, emotions are carefully restrained without any drama. Dasgupta writes,

> Sita's sisters shut their eyes
> Sita's sisters had eyeless holes
> Sita's sisters cried out to their mother earth
> "Remember our sister Sita's suicide,
> Innocent Sita's traumatic trials
> O mother rescue us as you rescued Sita"

(Page 14)

There is no seething rage — but quiet fortitude. There is no crying or cursing, no self-pity, or palpable frustration. Despite the calculated restraint, the horror is stark in Sita's voice,

> Shunning further exhibitions of pristine,
> pious purity
> I have now entered my mother's healing bosom
> To be a queen had been traumatic
> and beyond all reason!

(Page 16)

There is dignity even in the face of apathy. All of which are conveyed succinctly through a powerful language. Even when Sita complains:

> But LuvaKusha long for their father
> Ram is their hero, their role model
> Me, Sita, their devoted mother
> I could never be their role model

(Page 16)

The hegemonic society has used the trope of golden deer to bait innumerable hapless women. Sita though the champion of women's rights criticizes herself when it comes to her obsession for the golden deer which is beyond what is ordained by Mother Nature. Further, she is the quintessential philosopher who ponders over the logic of the perennial subjection of woman as a means to an end – Helen, Sita, Draupadi, or the unborn female foetus – the list is long.

> Male authors of the world's patriarchal epics blame
> The bewitching femme fatales
> who seem bereft of shame
> But the heroes insist they need
> such beauties as their brides

> In the killing fields and theatres of war,
> like trophies
> By their sides.

(Page 18)

Sita's spirited riposte to women of substance is to realize that deification is but a patriarchal ploy at comprehending, nay taming woman's enigmatic blend of beauty that is kept beyond bounds with the armour of knowledge and power. Dasgupta thus attempts not just a radical displacement of the focus of the poem from patriarchal/chauvinistic social ethos but catapults the text on a universal eco-feminist plane by proclaiming through it the 'Sitaness' of her sisters— "Rita, Mita, Arpita, Sumita, Rinita / Lolita, Bonita, Anita, Sunita, Sucheta" (Page 13). Sita and her sisters transcend all space-time bounds; as one recognizes the all too relevant efforts at gender sensitization and valid probe of the patriarchal politics of deification. The poet urges her readers "to read these poems as texts of resistance and resilience, confidently gesturing towards inevitable social change." She scripts *ecriture feminine* by demystifying the epic language and creates a discourse that easily crisscrosses time and space.

Dasgupta is noticeably free from either the Bloomean 'anxiety of influence' or the hallowed epic device of invoking a muse, she shows subaltern agency through a radically subversive reading of accepted facts from the female point of view, armed with the neo-historicist tool that at once destroys periodicity through assimilation from what is called 'a timeless history.' We thus have a Sita who dwells alike in the corridors of power, in our households, streets, and calls centres, in the victimhood of a Nirbhaya, in the helpless tears and hidden fears of the poor or even in the innumerable single mothers who battle for legal rights and social acceptance of their children! The twenty-first century Sita, as Dasgupta writes, is "… not Lakshmi Bound / I am Lakshmi Unbound"(Page 19). That this is no romantic demagoguery but the poet's exhortation of womanhood to reassess in the light of Sita their steely resolve is made clear.

As a true feminist she is aware of what is happening in and around. She voices her concern for Kashmir in "Heaven on Earth" and "The Valley of Fear." "Who Killed the Little Tribal Girl?" a voice of protest and resistance shows how patriarchy, which is an embedded social structure, tries to legitimize gender violence and how the ancestry of such legitimizing may undeniably be found in the ancient epic forms that Dasgupta here tries to interrogate. This little tribal girl remains as a sharp reminder of the place as well as space, within the narrative, of the incarceration of helpless tribal kids/ women who have practically no recourse to anything which is called humanity.

> They said, "these unruly tribal kids
> She must have been killed by a pack of wild dogs
> These filthy low-caste pests are such scums
> They claim our land and blame us
> when they die!"(Page 73)

Some of the poems in this collection namely— "Easter in Krakow," "Park Street," "A Failed Dream," do not have a feminist slant in them. "My Mother's Harmonium" is intensely personal. "Calcutta/Kolkata," "two in one: Calcutta" speaks of her love for the city.

In poems like "Cows Blazing" and "The Dumb Cow," she scathingly criticizes the present situation of the country. The poem "Protest" speaks of a silent presence where one feels nude, defenseless, with a grim cordon of fear "and not a single voice rises in protest" (Page 76). Sita/Dasgupta in this collection of poetry virtually overturns the Aristotelian definition of catharsis as pity and fear inspired by the odious fate of 'one like ourselves'; rather she posits herself as indelible and through her ideal, fosters a bond of solidarity for all her sisters across the spectrum of space and time.

Title: *Sita's Sisters*
Author: Sanjukta Dasgupta
Page: 80
ISBN: 978-93-87883-89-5
Edition: Paperback, 2019
Published by Hawakal Publishers, India.
Price: INR 300 | USD 11.99

Selected Songs: Rabindranath Tagore

In the introduction to the volume:*Selected Songs: Rabindranath Tagore,* translated by Aditya Kumar Deva Majumdar, the editor, noted poet, Gopal Lahiri writes, "Rabindranath Tagore often feels that songs are his best creations. He said that his songs would live long when all his other works were buried and forgotten. Many believe that Tagore's creative journey resonates more with his songs than anything else." This is true to the core, for *Rabindrasangeet* ran the entire gamut of human emotion, ranging from his early dirge-like Brahmo devotional hymns to songs of nature, patriotic songs, love songs, and miscellaneous. Sometimes Tagore's songs emulated the tonal colour of classical ragas to a great extent. It is in his songs that Tagore undertakes a journey to the world of revelatory radiance.

Aditya Kumar Deva Majumdar was born in 1882 in Allahabad. He completed his M.A. in literature from Allahabad University. He started his career as a teacher in a school and later served as Head Master in Govt. High School, Muzaffarnagar, UP on the British Government pay scale as a special case. His notable works include the English translation of 153 songs and verses of Rabindranath Tagore which he had noted down in a small diary in his handwriting. He passed away in 1978 at the age of 96. The present volume saw the light of the day due to the untiring efforts of his daughter Mita Das Majumdar now residing at Vadodara. The intention being to reach out to a larger audience for reference and appreciation.

The slim edition is bilingual, each fragment of translated text paired with its original on the facing page. Adita Kumar Deva Majumdar's translation into English of Rabindranath Tagore's timeless Bangla original text of *Rabindrasangeet* is skillful. He has been able to replicate the swift-flowing lucidity and charm of the original Bangla songs by Tagore. The success of a translated text is its readability. This is undoubtedly the acid test. Aditya Deva Majumdar's translation of Tagore's songs into English has passed that test with flying colours. The readers both at home and in the world, that is specifically those readers who are unable to read the Bengali language will be grateful to the translator for enabling them to read these Tagore's songs in English translation.

The tapestry of Tagore's songs is woven with a preponderance of Hindusthani classical music, Carnatic Classical, select Western. It is replete with Bengali folk culture and traditions, the flavour of which is local cultural connotation. Aditya Deva Majumdar has captured every nuance of the original songs of Tagore and negotiated without undermining the innate rhythm and essence of Tagore. Like the translation "To The Pilgrim,"

> How dismal dark is night,
> All blotted out of sight
> Pilgrim, Where alone guest prithee say
> Through the dark woody way? (Page 31)

This reads almost like Tagore. Aditya Deva Majumdar manages to keep the lyrical tremor, rhyme, cadence, and the creative universe of the poet admirably. What is more remarkable is that he has given title to each song. The editor writes, "I have made allowances by not altering words / phrases or polishing the texts in order to make them modern and feel good and keep them as it is barring unavoidable editing to retain the older charm of Tagore era." He further writes, "I am glad to bring this brilliant work to the readers even though there is not much of information relating to the context and personal notes available in the manuscript and some of his writings are not clearly readable."

The editor Gopal Lahiri has authored seven volumes in English and published across various anthologies as well as in eminent journals of India and abroad. He has deftly chosen fifty songs of Tagore for the collection. It comprises of devotional, love, nature, patriotic and miscellaneous— 'Puja,' 'Prem,' 'Prakriti,' 'Swadesh' and 'Bibidha.' These songs offer solace and a sense of connection with the outer world.

> I play with you the tuneful play, / It is a far
> off play; In morning time, the tune of pain

/ My flute hath 'gun to play. / When with you, My Lord, come yourself / And seize my flute and on its play, / And through the stillness of dark night / Bring your song into play? (Page 73)

Thus these selected songs are not only appealing but connect the commoners as well as the connoisseurs. There is a general feeling that translation of words will not be enough to translate songs of Tagore because they are more rooted in the soil, to the people and culture of Bengal. What is laudable is that the translator has made every effort to make his translations closer to the original, with a natural flavour and more nuanced in English, keeping the rhymes in an orderly manner. As Tagore is a master of metaphor, it is often difficult to identify the true meaning that underlies the texts, Aditya Deva Majumdar is quite successful in capturing Tagore's brilliance in his translations. What is truly great about Tagore is that his songs are identifiable with every mood, with every situation. "In fact, Tagore wants to communicate to the outside world through his songs and he brings that timbre so brilliant to life." Aditya Deva Majumdar has tried to capture the essence in his translations.

In modern times, regional languages are usually neglected, a unique way of preserving the regional languages and regional literature that are being gulped by the all-powerful English language is to use English translations to sustain local cultures and practices. It has been noticed that nowadays children and youth shy away from developing reading and writing skills of vernacular texts. They feel that vernacular texts are inferior in nature and quality. They prefer translated texts. This collection will cater to their needs too. Hope that this competent translation of Tagore's songs will be read by lay readers of translated texts along with researchers on Tagore. The editor deserves a special mention for unearthing this treasure trove for us.

Tittle: Selected Songs: Rabindranath Tagore
Translated by: Aditya Kumar Deva Majumdar
Editor: Gopal Lahiri
Page: 112
ISBN: 978-93-88815-77-2
Edition: Hardbound, January 2020
Published by Abhijan Publishers, Kolkata, India.
Price: Rs 200 | USD 10

Alike but Apart: a review of *Rituals*

Introducing *Rituals*, the formidable poet Dustin Pickering writes, "Ritual, properly understood, signifies gratitude and is rooted in the habitual nature of the human organism." Kiriti Sengupta's collection of poetry is a search. What he is seeking through *Rituals* is not a disembodied spirit, but one with a distinct, beautiful form. The spirit is the rituals itself. The poetry mesmerizes. Kiriti Sengupta who has been awarded the *Rabindranath Tagore Literary Prize* 2018 for his contribution to literature is a dental surgeon, poet, editor, translator, and publisher from Kolkata. He has several books to his credit, *Healing Waters Floating Lamps, The Earthen Flute, Reflections on Salvation, The Unheard, Solitary Stillness, Dreams of the Sacred and Ephemeral*, being a few.

Rituals are *manodharma* (*manas*, literally mind, and *dharma*, which is an exploration of the ethical within one's being. *Rituals* (2019), Sengupta's recent collection of poetry is an instrument of critical inquiry, also of life.

"Comeback," the opening poem of the collection, whispers, "I return after a year ... My tired eyes uncover the kohl of night, while my glasses spot tears" (Page 17). This does not happen every day. It happens when there is an emotion when there is creativity. The lines are not a rigid structure: they allow the freedom to explore. The creative also implies ethics. As one explores the poetical history of the form of *Rituals*—the technical detailing, melodic, textual, and rhythmic intricacies and their histories, one realizes that none of these aspects of an art form can be divorced from the social, philosophical, and political constructs that govern every interior poetical movement. The poet says, "Timing is crucial, to say the least" (Page 23). He wants to collapse the distinction between genres, questioning the politics of even the nomenclature. Thus he freely writes, "Patrons do not frequent ageing accolades anymore... An appraiser is called out to rouse commendation" (Page 25).

There is something called ethical art and that comes from working through the cobwebs of societal restrictions. Sengupta's poetry exists within art forms and between art forms. Thus when he thinks of an alternative view as "When God is a Woman," he writes, "How many householders meet in / a whorehouse? / How many *mujras* dwell in a *kotha*? Like her admirers / God is silent / In her sinews / hides a hint of soil / from the yard of courtesans" (Page 27). We are aware of the age-old ritual of bringing in a palm-full of soil from the household of the lesser daughters of Durga during the construction of the idol of Goddess. Thus the poem is an attempt at an exploration of the ethical that rituals (*Rituals*) are and a quest for equality. The poet has attempted to free the art. Gnosis must meet praxis. Art must be revisited—and reformed. So Sengupta has taken his poetry to the unlikeliest of places, the brothel. The poem is remarkably powerful and draws the attention of the readers to the rituals which we follow religiously. The poem is a metaphor for almost everything that is marginalized and neglected: spaces, people, poetry.

"Male" speaks of a space that remains invisible, "I find myself connected / when my child says Baba. / Moments of intimacy surface / when my wife wants me to listen. / Mother makes sense / when she calls me son / Performing the last rites / adds to the legacy" (Page 31). Language and culture conspire in such a way to maintain social hierarchies, thus by dedicating the book to the "Bauls" who practice the "other" form of music against the "classical" Sengupta is perhaps questioning the definitions such as "classical" or "folk." This is also a kind of a ritual to pay homage to the wandering minstrels of rural Bengal. For the sensitive poet customs and rituals "are like mediation— / worthy of unhurried contemplation" (Page 35).

In *Rituals*, the poet gravitates towards a subject that has a message in a subliminal way. In "Timings", he writes, "It's difficult to sever amity / even if it fails / A new friend splits the bond faster. / Why do we hold stars / responsible for the rift? / Once in a while, / it is crucial to get cornered. / That's when / I touch / the fiber of camaraderie." On the other hand, the poem

"Religion" (Page 49) brings us the true meaning of religion. The readers get into layers of this poem and it is a richer experience. One absorbs a message from it, it stays with us for days and weeks. This exactly is what Sengupta's poetry can do, it weaves the kind of value that can be created. In today's world, it might be too pompous for a poet to claim that poetry can bring about a change. But one strongly believes that there are a sustained number of poems in this collection of poetry that speak about a certain issue and add value to it. In crisp lines the poet makes us realize the reality: "Relax! Bumps help us realize the earth" (Page 53). "Patience" advises one to "ignore all coercions" for one has to remember that "Roots penetrate concrete / until they are exercised" (Page 55).

There is a strange naivety in the poem "After the Book Fair." The poem speaks of a different kind of ritual. Once the book fair is over there is an inevitable relief, there is a routine cleaning up. The authors, the sellers, publishers store their books and look for a new venue. The poem speaks of the everyday mundane ritual which is a mixture of hope, restoration, and conclusiveness. "From the shelves, new hope will follow the merchandise" (Page 91). "Masala Muri" illustrates how it is representative of the Indian culture and tradition. Sengupta recognizes that this simple delicacy is of immense importance in the lives and lifestyles of people of Indian descent like him. Through puffed rice or *masala muri* (muri is a traditional Bengali snack), the Indian culture continues to be strong and vibrant. The poem embodies the representations of food, traditions, celebrating the rituals. The poet voices forth spiritedly the heartfelt emotions and experiences of the colourful Indian culture and ethos.

The poet then adds on to our experience: "Rituals do not add to our credos," for "Indianness precedes theology." The experience becomes transnational. Thus, identities are intimately connected to the concepts of cultural identity and nation. As Stuart Hall comments, identity is not as transparent or unproblematic. Perhaps, instead of thinking of identity as an already accomplished fact, which the new cultural practices then represent, Sengupta's poetry insists that identity should be thought of as a "production" which is never complete, always in process, and always constituted within, representation. Cultural identity, in this sense, is a matter of becoming, as well as of being. It belongs to the future as well as to the past. It is not something that already exists, transcending place, time, history, and culture. Cultural identities come from somewhere, have histories. But, like everything historical, they undergo constant transformation. Identities are the names we give to the different ways we are positioned by, and position ourselves within, the narratives of the past.

The final poem "Exhibition" reminds one of Shelley's *Ozymandias* where the traveller finds a broken statue of a legendary king of ancient time, lying forgotten in the desert, with these words carved on its base:" My name is Ozymandias, king of kings: Look on my works, ye Mighty, and despair! Sengupta's traveller finds that the various artifacts are missing their noses! The poet adopts a subtle way to deflate human pride. "I think of effigies with fractured noses/ …Nature made the nasal frame fragile. / How do they breathe the vain air? (Page 99). The poet reminds us that power is only temporary. Earthly power is mutable, and indeed all human beings need to remember this. There is no place for pride and arrogance in Nature.

In his search for life, the poet seems to implore the spirit of rituals to appear. There is magic in his verses. The verses will surely make the readers explore their rituals. Sengupta's *Rituals* add to the oeuvre of Indian poetry in English. The illustrations by Partha Pratim Das are an added embellishment to the collection of poetry.

Title: *Rituals*
Author: Kiriti Sengupta
Page: 99
ISBN: 978-93-87883529
Edition: Hardbound | Paperback, 2019
Published by Hawakal Publishers, India
Price: INR 300 | USD 10.99

Pain and Paradox:
a review of *Banaras And The Other*

Ashwani Kumar is a poet, author, and professor of Development Studies at Tata Institute of Social Sciences. Presently, he is a Senior Fellow of the Indian Council of Social Science Research. *Banaras And the Other* is his second collection of poems after his first anthology, *My Grandfather's Imaginary Typewriter*, published by Yeti Books. Banaras (officially Varanasi) is one of the oldest cities in the world. It is perhaps one of the few sites that have witnessed continuous habitation from ancient times. Even during the lifetime of the Buddha, it was a flourishing city. No wonder that it evokes images of the universal, the timeless, and the cosmic, and is deeply embedded in the consciousness of an average Hindu. The book under review is set out to demystify and deromanticize Banaras. Banaras, thus, continues to remain a case study of the challenges to be met in an attempt to archaeologically unearth the past religious traditions of a living city that claims primordial antiquity. While discussing Banaras as a Hindu, Buddhist, and Jain holy city, one should not lose sight of the fact that Muslims have resided in the city since at least the 13th century. Ashwani Kumar's *Banaras And The Other* is thus a welcome addition to the body of Indian English poetry that seeks to enhance one's awareness of the past and the present.

The book has a taut structure and is divided into five sections—Banaras, Nostalgia of Ugly Days, The Architecture of Alphabetical Order, Myths Monsters and Fake Heroes, and Submission to the Good Barbarian. The poet begins with an "Overture to Banaras by Jatin Das." The lead poem, "Anatomy of Baranassey As Told by Major James Rennell," seems to embody a paradox. The protagonist Major Rennell, Surveyor-General and author of "Bengal Atlas (1779), is a historical character whose fictional journey from Lat Bhairav riots of 1809 to electoral insurgencies of Hindutva in 2014 illustrates the 'pain and paradox' in contemporary India as K. Satchidanandan mentioned in the blurb for the book. It is a cartographic poem, mapping rising cases of Xenophobia, Islamophobia, and homophobia.

> Bathed in sun and salt,
> draped in a white loincloth,
> she enters the perineum
> of the sanctum sanctorum of
> the buffalo-horned masked ascetic God. (Page 3)

We are all aware that lately, Banaras has become a political fantasy for Hindutva politics. Ironically, the more swatches (clean) it becomes, the more exclusivist and intolerant it is. References to real persons and events are purely accidental and imaginary. But they are rooted in the 'fissured, schismatic scenarios of 21st century India,' as Ranjit Hoskote has noted.

> We were warned by the famous local bard,
> "One half of the city lives in water:
> the other half is a dead body (shava)" (Page 5)

Ashwani is using Banaras as a site and text to expose the fake spiritual gurus and corporate spiritual trainers. In this poem, Hinduism is a deeply engrained living faith without any ethnic markers or cultural barriers; it is a fluid, mellifluous universal music of love and peace. In contrast, Hindutva is a politics of religion and state power.

> A new republic had dawned on the holy town.
> With black ink on the index finger,
> unbaptized Hindus, prime-time anarchists,
> part-time secularists and the
> famous Internet Baba had assembled
> on the banks of the polluted Himalayan river,
> and promised to clean accumulated ancient filth.
> (Page 5)

Appearing in most grand, seductive, perhaps sexy ways, these new-Gods(?) preside over an illusory world of 'lies, more lies,' and command so-called 'cobalt truth' in various parts of the world. Thus Ashwani's reference to the 'great leader, in golden Afghan jacket limited-edition watch and Deccan rubber shoes' is allegorical and metaphorical. It alludes to the phenomena of return of primordial patriarchs leading irrational and uncontrollable blood-thirsty mobs in their pursuits of power. This phenomenon of 'great leader' has been the focus of recent writings of Pankaj Mishra, Tabish Khair, Basharat Peer, and others. Thus *Banaras* works at multiple levels; it is part historical, part mnemonic, and mostly fictional retelling of Banaras, the seat of Lord Siva, and the holiest cremation ground of Hindus. Banaras is also imagined as a beautiful woman whose sensuous, divine love has been immortalized in *thumris* sung by Siddeshwari Devi, Rasoolan Bai, and Girija Devi, and other great singers.

> Everyone, including junkies,
> smashed their looms in Shiva's city
> And hid themselves in the ninety-nine epithets
> of Allah (Page 7)

Banaras resists binaries because it has many selves, eternal and ephemeral, primitive and modern, ascetic, and hedonistic at the same time. It is sublime and filthy, sexual and so deeply spiritual. For the poet, Banaras is not only the seat of Lord Siva but also 'Kaaba of Hindustan.'

Ashwani further dedicates a poem to his mother, from the next section— "Nostalgia of Ugly Days"— in which he recounts a personal spiritual experience. As a young boy, he had witnessed,

> Beneath the underground sky,
> She stored terracotta of tall men with
> Dry mutton kebabs,
> Whenever seven old monks,
> Snakes slithering
> Through their adulterous flesh,
> visited our house,

They found her making love
to the Sun God at the Golan Heights. (Page13)

The next section, "The Architecture of Alphabetical Order," captures the various moods of the poet—personal and political, memories and nostalgia. "Myths, Monsters and Fake Heroes" deal with mythical characters and contemporary parodies. There is an intersection, if not altogether a confluence, of Eastern and Western traditions in the practice of writing poetry, Ashwani curiously inherits both the traditions through the mediations of colonial and global cultures one after the other. In this context, if we read Ashwani's *Banaras* which is a book of prose poems, we are indeed reading an example of the said intermingling. It is to be noted that it is not only the mixing of Eastern and Western literary traditions but also mixing prose and poetry, the mixing of Indian and Western cultures. "Yudhishthira's Kala Kutta" (dedicated to Arun Kolatkar) belongs to the lineage whose ancestor had a link with *The Mahabharata*. The poem highlights the change that the colonial period has brought into India. The dog is considered to be man's best companion for ages.

...We came here
With our five brothers. Four of them had no
Names of their own, so they were called by their
Employers: hawker, barber, tailor, bangle-seller.
Only Yudhistira, who never lied,
Followed his family name and occupation...
...After years of struggle in
fag-ashed denim trousers,
Without any worldly possessions,
The brothers fell one by one
on the road to Himalaya.

Only Yudhistira's black dog Bruno,
Survived the hardships of displacements
(Page 54-55)

In "Something Is Rotten In the State of Denmark," he juxtaposes King Yayati, the first King of Pandavas with Hamlet, the Prince of Denmark, the result is a mischievous irreverence. "Job Interview At The Clinic of Doctor Faustus" is sarcastic in tone. "Brihannala in Dadar Ladies Bar" is a poem that is perhaps the best in the entire collection. The poet writes,

...I don't want to become Arjuna, again,
A blind carnivorous beast who
Killed his own cousins, nephews and
Teachers in the age of darkness (Page 68)

He thus dexterously sums up the essential teachings from *The Mahabharata*, which provides its readers with the ultimate philosophy behind life and living.

Today, nobody knows my whereabouts,
Some say I am still working at
Dadar Dance Bar.(Page 71)

This poem can be compared to an image, and the reader must possess the eye to comprehend the original piece of literature through the image. One is immediately reminded of Plato's "Theory of Forms or Ideas." It is a morsel that can be masticated for a long. Just like writing, reading too is a lonely pursuit until there is "illumination":

Others say I was last seen doing a fusion pole dance
in the holy gardens of Addis Ababa. (Page 71)

The last section of this collection, "Submission To the Good Barbarian," and the last poem, "Fascism,

Fascism, Fascism," works its way where words are absent and make space for the loudness of thought. Ashwani not only replays the affront but also makes the moot point, almost in the manner of a metaphysical conceit that effects a shock,

> The idea was to arouse hatred and
> thirst for blood to gain insight
> into the innocence of our evil
> actions (Page 75)

In a way, the poems in this collection have no stable poetic forms and often migrate in unpredictable and whimsical ways. It is paradoxical —physical and mystical like conjoined twins. Ashwani's poems blur prose-poetry boundaries and create something like hybrid spaces where one does not worry about the craft in the conventional sense. This is what poets call the highest form of beauty in which "what eats is eaten, / and what is eaten, eats / in turn." (*Taittirya Upanishad*)!

Title: *Banaras And The Other*
Author: Ashwani Kumar
Pages: 95
ISBN: 978-93-82749-56-1
Edition: Paperback, 2017
Published by Paperwall Media & Publishing Pvt. Ltd.
Mumbai. India
Price: INR 240 | USD 14

Bridging the Gaps

The editors, Sharmila Ray and Gopal Lahiri, make it clear at the beginning of this anthology that they are not going to bore the readers with a foreword or introduction, they do not want their readers to read poetry through their minds. Rather they would love to include the readers and their different interpretations as a part of this anthology, unseen but vibrant and vibrating. The title *Bridging Continents: An Anthology of Indo-American Poets* is significant and apt. Poetry is a bridge and the poems of the twenty poets bridges one continent to another, one person to another, one time to another. Standing on a threshold we expect that poetry can change us. Both the continents America and India have a rich literary lineage, and "Bridging Continents" is the bridge through which readers walk the course.

The Anthology opens with the poetry of Alan Britt. His opening poem "Western Music" is led by the creative impulse of the talented Mozart and driven by the youthful verve of Beethoven, the poem is an attempt to venture into uncharted territory for both the talented musicians with the verses eschewing the world and its myriad cares to delve into the troubled minds of two individuals. "The Daffodils" of Andrea Witzke Slot evokes a series of nightmarish situations where the human spirit, symbolized by the recurrent image of daffodils, is crushed by monstrous creatures that stand for the vicious agents of humanity. Her spare lines forcefully evoke the agony and the trauma of human beings in oppressive situations down the ages. Ayaz Rasool Nazki's "Morning At A Dying Lake" speaks of nature in all her temperamentality and shifting moods. "The wide green lotus leaf / Like a cradle holds / A bunch of crystals / Sparkling up into blue sky / As rows upon rows of lotus / Stand guard to last secrets of the lake" (Page 24).

Bibhu Padhi's verses in "Stranger in the House," "Poem for my Son," "Listening through the Rain" are fluid lines that etch out a lifetime. "Today / the rains are once again here, / and I can almost remember / your wet voice / through my son's loud singing, / through the humming sound / of motor cars crowding the road / and, beyond all this." Dah Helmer's poem "A Night of Radiant Beauty" is one of deep contemplation and the evanescence of life and volatility of nature. Gjek Marinaj is a poet, writer, literary critic, and founder of the Protonism Theory. He has stepped away from established isms to embrace new practices and stake out unchartered territory. He does not use poetry as a mute surface but gets inside the fibre of poetry to engage in a partnership with it, exploring its diversity, its tactile richness, its plastic possibilities. Marinaj romances the medium and turns it into the message: the words and verses that he makes become a sentient material of disturbing implications as he articulates subtle inflections in it. He thus writes: "Unconcerned for the desperate comets panting up yonder, / At once, like a flowery honey-drenched dream, entered the bold / New evening, and undid the top two buttons of her black shirt: / And for us she hung on her neck the moon washed in gold." (Page 38). Heath Brougher's poems are an intriguing and layered narrative that swells with hope and despair, with a considerable measure of humour thrown in.

In his poems "Whirlpools," "My Hills, My Valleys," "The Stone Carver" H. K. Kaul turns ecstatic, lugubrious, positive, morbid, maudlin, and a whole lot of other things, as he negotiates a relationship with his readers. Jaydeep Sarangi in "Lake of the Mind" whips up a frenzy of lines to create an arboreal universe heaving with life where Rhododendron sanctuary is the embodiment of nature's creativity itself. In the lake of his mind, he has a liberating vision, for it hints at the possibility of the renewal of life itself. "But mind knows another story / Calm like Lachung river / Emptying into Teesta in a virgin dawn" (Page 50). The effect is one of deep contemplation and the evanescence of life and the volatility of nature. Mandira Ghosh in "I" begins to answer fundamental questions such as where she has come from and where she has to ultimately reach in search of identity. "I can't wait, I can't wait / Eternity calls me / I move on / I move on / Or, every corpuscle

/ And over every living cell/ I can lie, I can rest." (52). Martha Collins speaks of a new space, a field of vision in her poem "Field." Michael Miassian romances the medium called poetry and turns it into the message: the words that he makes become a sentient material of disturbing implications as he articulates subtle inflections in it. "You, who could never / wrap your mind around / the idea of reincarnation / can now remember you other / lives, yes even the ant / and the elephant. / And now you wonder, / what is it that is coming next." (Page 60).

Parneet Jaggi's poems "Love Transforms," "Space" lay bare the poet's psyche. Her verses are pervaded by a sense of brooding contemplation. I "Love Transforms," she writes, "Mind waits not for the lover to appear and make love / Pain within carries the strength / enough to move the planets / This is how love transforms" (Page 64). Pradeep Biswal, Rainer Shulte, Frederick Turner have charmed the readers through their natural lyricism of poetic movements and touches to keep the poetry unpredictable. "Volume" of Sanjeev Sethi is a masterwork of technique and form for its complete rejection of all superfluous details in the composition. "Accoutred in platinum they were parked in a rococo / berg resort. They liquored up on premium swigs and / bounced to current beats with heavyweights from / across the big blue marble. Three hundred television / stations plus other media certified it as the wedding / of the year" (Page 76). Sanjukta Dasgupta's poems are deeply philosophical. "If Winter Comes" is poised between argument and empathy. She weaves a dream-like yarn here. In "Autumn" there is a sense of isolation, the fluid lines are spontaneous yet fitful. She thus writes:

"Autumn prepares me with compassion / For the everlasting hibernation / For Winter now tiptoes close behind" (Page 81).

Scott Thomas Outlar's poems speak of the poet's struggle to overcome the hurdles to be himself in a restless world. Sunil Sharma in "Water Dear" has shifted his focus to the tremendous, mysterious life force that nature is and its formidable power to create and to destroy. "Thin pale-faced rivers gasp / and ponds die daily, as cities move upwards / in a smoggy sky / and grey clouds are now very rare in a June / July sky of / Delhi" (Page 88). Memory is a motif in Vinita Agrawal's "What Lies in Stock" as part of her assertion of identity chequered by deletions and insertions induced by compulsions in her motherland. "What lies in stock after festive spring has gone / Or a lost sweet memory for which we mourn." Gopal Lahiri's Poems forays into diverse disciplines pick what can be termed collateral scraps to conjure a tenuous art of ideas, excerpts, and improvisation. An art without labels and firm boundaries that seek to trace patterns of unbidden, formless flow within an amorphous form. "The temple bell unsettles our dream on the edge of wilderness and the sound crosses the fanning coconut palm out into the distant sea."

shorebirds
fly over the
coconut palm (Page 101)

Sharmila Ray in "Home" deals with the concept of home. A home provides shelter. Paradoxically, it can also fragment. Resolutions need to be sought within these binaries. She probes and discovers, questions, and contemplates, conjuring worlds of thought. "As street lamps come to life in the evening and light from the sky dims, one realizes home is a single flickering glow within us" (Page 104). The editors, Gopal Lahiri and Sharmila Ray, through their poems and in editing the anthology have achieved something extraordinary, this meticulously crafted anthology is much more than an attempt at bridging the gap between the two continents. With the Bengali translations deftly done by poet Tanmoy Chakraborty *Bridging Continents* is going to be a new kind of anthology with a wider readership.

Title: *Bridging Continents*:
    an anthology of Indo-American poets
Editors: Sharmila Ray, Gopal Lahiri
Page: 134
ISBN: 978-81-939828-6-0
Edition: Paperback, 2019
Published by Zahir Publication, Kolkata, India
Price: Rs 350 | USD 5

Waltz to Life: a review of *Dancing the Light*

When two authors unconnected culturally, geographically, historically, or socially of two poetry-rich nations come together to play with unlimited possibilities of the joy and mirth of life, a literary fusion is destined to happen. *Dancing the Light: an anthology of Indo-Australian poets*, edited by Rob Harle and Jaydeep Sarangi, and published by Cyberwit.net, carries in its pages, that stomp of the unexpected and unlimited joys of life. This is the seventh book in their Australian-Indian poetry series published by Cyberwit. The previous anthologies are *Poetic Connections: Poems From Australia and India*, (Lonsdale); *Building Bridges: Poems From Australia and India*, (Harle); *Voices Across The Ocean: Poems From Australia and India*, (Harle& Sarangi); *Homeward*

Bound: Poems From Australia and India (Sarangi & Harle); *The Land: Poems From 6 Australia and India* (Sarangi & Harle) *Searching For the Sublime* (Sarangi & Harle).

The theme of this anthology is *Dancing Light*. Dancing is a metaphor for celebration, enjoyment, transporting one to that special place; Light is of course a metaphor for brightness, clarity, seeing clearly, enlightenment. Poems in this anthology are a record of deep-seated questioning minds carrying reverberations within. These intimate poems manifest the truth through unique images from life, death, the rain, and so on. In the introduction to this anthology, the editors make it clear: "We wanted this collection to have a positive feel and outcome, no doom and gloom poems dwelling solely on Extinction, Anthropocene Depression, Climate Change Disaster or the woes of the world." Hence the poets — eleven Indian poets and eleven Australians, create a much-expanded understanding of the notion of the positive side of life in their works.

The Anthology opens with "kaleidoscopically colouring memories /, pirouetting moments" of life. "Botticelli Dances with Venus" (Page 10) looks far beyond geographical boundaries and the poet Adrian Rogers extends his field of vision to include the 'dying sun' 'above the horizon.' It is thrilling to catch Amelia Walker's "Sky Dance": Hot night, storms brewing/, the clouds fox-trot, / slow then faster, / their arms glistening bolts of lightning, / their hearts the beating thunder (Page 18). Sky comes to the earth and dances with life sprinkled with joy. "Lessons in Dancing" (Page 19) offers a rewarding experience by teaching us the lessons of life, "most of us hated poetry and dancing and later, / some of us turned to jazz, to rap, / to punk, not realizing / these were their own forms / of poetry / and poetry its own kind / of dance"(Page 19-20). Basudhara Roy catapults her verses to an elevated plane and reminds us of keeping the door of life ajar, "I do not know / if, when you leave, you think / of me. It does not matter. / All that matters is this door ajar" (Page 29). In "Journeys" (Page 31), she plays with unlimited possibilities of experience to mould its performance for newer goals in life. Brian Dally wary us of our pride and arrogance at a moment when man thinks he has made giant leaps in science "in the end we're here for one brief dance, and then we're gone, but love and life and death will carry on" (Page 36).

Bronwyn E Owen in "Healing" pens an aesthetic experience an enriching encounter with nature: "the trees said to me / I am my own guru / and so are you I didn't understand then / I understand now" (Page 40). Cameron Hindrum slips in some secrets of life to his readers in "What Will Survive Us": "The age of no turning back / – On which we have all turned our backs. / Walking leads me through this quiet / Until I can find the river again: / Which, at least, is honest" (Page 54). Christopher (Kit) Kelen is a twelve-piece poem "Hardanger Set" sheds bits of imagery, leaving faint, teasing clues of life, "Have a head of song. / Imagine yourself never touching at all. / That's insect, bird, and angel business. / The one breath. / It's so much distance I'm thrown from. / Make the heart empty / Be whole" (Page 61). "Impossible Words" speak of poet David Hallett's intense engagement with the moment, but without attachment: "spoken in softest tones / at the break of day and the dawn of night / – impossible words: forever always and never – / to love and be loved (to love and be loved) / that is all" (Page 63). He has an epiphanic moment when he realizes it is only love which bridges the gap in life, "and there is a bridge, / a bridge leaps the waters and the tower of trees, / a bridge of dreams and words, / its path is fern and flower and golden rain, / and always, always the bridge is love" (Page 68).

D C Chambial's "Beautiful Beyond" is almost like a metaphysical devotional poem where the poet expresses his earnest desire to step back to a place where there is a beauty beyond "Serene Satisfaction, sans deeds, Writ large on every face" (Page 71). Gopal Lahiri's verses have a unique serenity that calms the soul. A true clairvoyant he writes: "The invitation is always there to transcend time, / Creating the healing space in nature / In search of the truth" (Page 78). "Armistice" (Page 81) remains an aesthetic treat for the readers and "Dancing Light" wrapped in hope speaks of his *oeuvre*. Janie Conway Herron's poem "Winter Nights" (Page 84) is a treat to the senses. There is a neatness in "Home"– "That silent place / where my own words / flow" (Page 85) which adds a rare verve to the poem. Jaydeep Sarangi's poems "Truth" and "A Poem Away" have a magnetic pull because of the element of drama in them. He writes, "I want to be a river, someday when my prayers will be done" (Page 95). His soft focus is life, human life with its myriad hues, their substance, liquefied in dappled tones.

Laxman Singh Rathore in his poem seeks divine blessings from "The Being who possesses neither name Nor form, / nor a fixed domain Divine Glimpses (Page 102). Malaswami Jacob recreates old Mizo folklore about the journey of the spirits of the dead to the other world

(Page 111-12). Some of the poems of Mark Cornell "Our Dusk Visitor," "Mr. Plover" are buoyed with quizzical humour. Nathalie Buckland in "Ordinary Miracles" (Page 127) writes about the binaries of individual identity and anonymity. PadmajaIyengar-Paddy's lyrical poems have a thematic structure of life perhaps trying to negotiate inexplicable buffetings, to remain anchored. She writes, "I felt a strange light pervading my whole being Meaning of Life I finally saw without really seeing..." (Page 138). The poems of Pankajam Kottarath reintroduce us to our experiences of life. There is a swift gliding in Paramita Mukherjee Mullick's "When I became Queen For a Day" (Page 150), feather-light bristles that arrest words in diverse splotches at places—favouring in both cases, chance over life.

Robert Madox Harle's meaningful verses "The Return," "Dancing the Light" are impregnated with the aches of existence, they are no doubt different for different people, the fissures that we create in life are filled up by poetry and its attendant virtues. He thus says, "the realization that everything is light, photons and pixels / dancing in harmony, / a Waltz in the zero-point-field. / If that's all there is, then let's keep dancing"(Page 159). Saima Afreen's poems in this collection are an exploration of the complexity of the cross-currents blowing across such heterogeneous spheres as society, polity, ecology, and economy. The poems "Of Dark Suns," "A Couplet" are steeped in life and its memories, the thoughts they evoke are diverse. Her verses are so engaging beyond her extraordinary virtuosity. Sunil Sharma's agile verses glide nimbly over the frets, *sans* any kind of visible effort or scraping. The lyrical phrasing "eyes closed, lips muttering hymns composed thousands of years before — and still sung with gusto in the middle-class homes believing in old gods, in a commercial city" (Page 170) brings out the poem's stunning simplicity, which makes it a modern classic. "Dancing Light" (Page 175-76) is embedded with its mounting melody hiding the daunting technical work it involves.

The editors of this anthology Rob Harle and Jaydeep Sarangi have daunted a formidable task. The task of the selection of poets to maintain a balance between gender, age, race, and personal ideologies. They have done it masterfully. Few could have done better than them. The poets too help the readers to broaden their horizons. This anthology will surely entice scholars, researchers, and students for a better understanding of the subtle nuances of life.

Title: *Dancing the the Light*
Author: Rob Harle & Jaydeep Sarangi
Page: 176
ISBN: 978-93-88125-90-1
Edition: Paperback, 2020
Published by Cyberwit.net. UP. India.
Price: INR 300

Memory Ecologies: A Review of Amit Shankar Saha's *Fugitive Words*

Fugitive Words is the second collection of poems (first being *Balconies of Time*) by Amit Shankar Saha, an award-winning poet, and short story writer. He is the co-founder of *Rhythm Divine Poets* and fiction editor of *Ethos Literary Journal.* As Dustin Pickering, in his foreword to the volume, describes, "Amit S. Saha explores memory and desire through the lens of loss and despair. The grief is beyond personal ... As we travel these poems, we are introduced to a scientific understanding that is compatible with humanist spirituality." Ra Sh in the blurb to the book writes, "Amit's poems in their journey with words and memories are not limited to any singular species of memories, but are drawn from many histories and geographies." The poems bring forth the literary mediation of memory and experience set in the narratives of a particular time, space and milieu. The understanding of memory mediated through the poems refers to a specific modality of reflection by which the poet examines lived experiences ingrained into poetry. The approach is to arrive at propositions which locate poetry as an archive for memory. In the poem "Paisley," Amit writes:

> You, who will find her one evening smiling
> at me, while wishing an untimely goodbye
> and leave me with you under a roof roofless,
> know her footsteps echo an ancient
> amnesia of the beginning where
> she left paisleys of footprints on the leaves
> for generations of my rebirth to see
> and not recognize the fossils of the past (Page 25)

Memory here is not referred to as an abstraction per se- but a way of passing through the empirical to prepare new entities of interpreting poetry. In the poem "Spices," Amit writes,

> In Paradise Pickle Factories
> smell of grandmothers sits
> cross-legged to tell stories
> of spices who went on long
> voyages across the seas.
> In that long long past
> Forefathers and foremothers
> of fenugreek and cardamom
> traded in gold and silver
> in the bazaars of Persia.

> ...Today in my turmeric mind
> when I recall their memory,
> listening to smells, smelling stories,
> tastes of a bay-leaf past
> seep in with all the oils and cloves. (Page 23)

It is important not to see memory as the inevitable result of merely an accumulation of data or information. The varied fields of poetic representations have changed the contours of memory formation and recognition which leads to new conceptual innovations and ideas. Another poem "Your Grandmother's Sari," speaks of his grandmother who has left many saris for his mother who wears them now. Along with the saris he is reminded of her habit of having betel nuts. The chief object of Amit's poem is to determine the relationship between the memory of the everyday experience, lived events, and its translation into poetry.

The poet stoically sits through the night reveals layers of personal passions, social insights, and aesthetic delight,

> If I remember you tonight,
> it is because my fugitive
> memory escapes the flaccid hours
> spent on the banks of forgetfulness. (Page 49)

The comparative study of both the written way of representing memory and reproduction of memory is the central argument here.

The poet is quite an expert in the economy of words carefully picking and choosing them. The words speak for more than the poet himself...

> my words, those that live in huts by the tracks,
> who own their lives in this light of dusk?
> They clamber into my poems
> like a broken bridge half-way into a river,
> like a broken roof half-way into a house. (Page 15)

These words are "fugitive words," they are literal fugitives, they escape the legal proceedings against them and find themselves rounded up in the verses.

> I have jailed my heart,
> no fugitive words
> will escape from it
> except in disguise
> like those trespassers. (Page 65)

The poet thus adopts a human approach to reach those dark fugitive lands of our essence. In this dark land, he speaks of rains,

> Two drops of water dribble
> And settle on a scooter seat but
> Their meniscuses don't meet.
> The days become wet and sticky
> Like folded damp paper.(Page 60)

In some of his poems like "This Bijoya," "Autumning," "Grey Love," "Rai," "Brinda," "Binodini," Amit does the "code-mixing," having a dialogue between Bengali and English words, which is integral to the ideas of the poem of place as well as identity. Words like "Bijoya," "Hemanta," "Rai," "Binodini," reflects the Indianness of the sociolinguistic trends in India. The long poem "Lahore Bomb Blast Series" speaks volumes, and pulls the heartstrings! "The

Hind Shawl Repairing House" is steeped in nostalgia and leaves the readers to ruminate. *Fugitive Words* use stored memory for future use and the poems in this collection act as a repository. Unlike a human mind, it is not prone to everyday degeneration. Through these acts, one visits revisit the past as well as the present and future. The artistic cover adds to the aesthetic pleasure of the reading experience.

Title: *Fugitive Words*
Author: Amit Shankar Saha
Page: 101
ISBN: 978-93-87883-69-7
Edition: Paperback, June 2019
Published by Hawakal Publishers, India
Price: INR 300 | USD 8.99

Lyrical Tide: a review of *Tidal Interlude*

Gopal Lahiri's poetry collection *Tidal Interlude* (2015) drifts the readers with emotional waves and the readers feel as if with the tide. He is such a poet who brings in a new perspective to the waves of life, trying to soak up the moment. Lahiri is a bilingual poet, writer, editor, critic, and translator and widely published in Bengali and the English language. He has had seven collections of poems in Bengali and English. He is the recipient of the Poet of the year and award in Destiny Poets, UK, 2016, and also received a featured poet award in Poetry In A Cup, USA, 2004, and a winner of Haiku in Poetry.com, USA, 2004. In the Introductory Note to the poetry collection, *Tidal Interlude*, Usha Kishore, the renowned poet writes, "Gopal Lahiri's current poetry collection, *Tidal Interlude* certainly conforms to Wordsworth's renowned definition of poetry. There is emotion here and amidst tranquil interludes, there is a powerful and spontaneous tide of feelings ... The collection highlights *panchabhuta* or the five elements of Indian philosophy and aesthetics: earth, water, air, fire, and sky. Lahiri's is a distinct elemental voice mapping the wilderness of the mind."

Nature has a special place in Lahiri's poems and the tide is a recurring motif that reflects the energy of swell and the inherent interlude. Tide is intrinsic in the periodic rise and fall of water and the overlapping moment breaks into lyrical music. Nature appeals to him which leaves the noise of the world behind and reconnects with the mosaic of words in his poems. *Tidal Interlude* is his third poetry collection after *Silent Steps* and *Living Inside*. Sunil Sharma, the noted poet writes: "With Gopal Lahiri, you hear each word speak clearly! The Mumbai-based earth-scientist is very sharp when it comes to crafting a tech report for the specialists or a sparkling poem for the connoisseurs. And each word counts in the composition: The dewy silence, clear crisp twilight, big skies, and empty landscapes — well, the words deployed are so every day and simple but undergo a quick metamorphosis in the poetic hands of Gopal and assume a special property called by consensus as lyrical!" Poems like "Secret Code," "Water," "My Space," are the reflections of an accomplished poet, who weaves a beautiful web of temporal spaces in contrasting shades of light and darkness. The poet deftly traverses a wide range of experiences and emotions.

Lahiri's verse is elegant that acmes convoluted craftsmanship: in the linear arrangement, in the syntactical ingenuity, and in the delicate literary devices that wing around like birds in flight.

> for now though,
> the optimum happiness signatures are those
> in the eyes of the rain-washed birds
> tempered with silken feathers and rummaged greenery.
> (Page 13)

The recurrent motif of birds, voice the poet's thoughts that read the unknown in the colours of the rainbow. Birds don the role of metaphysical conceits, while concurrently carrying out their flights and birdsong while being "tossed in the blue sky."

> The ringing sound of the distant temple bell,
> A link between the past and the primordial,
> Losing altitude the birds wind up their songs all too quickly" (Page 16)

The poetic persona is a "solitary bird making rounds in a way of finding the art of survival," providing occasional wingflashes of autobiographical feathers.

Tidal Interlude takes its readers by surprise at every corner. The poetry collection has pulsating tracts of resistance: in references to injustice, in allusions to past pain, in endeavours to break walls of silence and glass doors. The transferral in emphasis from philosophic replication to recalcitrant angst is dramatic:

> Now my hands are chopped, my skin is burnt, my face is blackened
> "Do not wash me in holy water
> I cannot join in your prayer in the temple." (Page 18)

"The starry night / Silent and still,
Burdened with mystery and milky ways,
Told more than you could tell" (Page 22)

The words deployed here are so every day and unassuming but undergo a nippy metamorphosis in the expressive hands of Lahiri and assume a lyrical perspective. His genius as an acute observer of the common, everyday, the ordinary and aestheticizing those tiny bits and remains into surprising metaphors and images and words that spark like the fireflies in the scented dark of a verdant valley.

"Let go of the past and move on.
The wall clock reminds...
Entice the sky to come down to this beautiful earth."
(Page 24)

The poet is fascinated by history and people. There is an exemplary dexterity, there are a certain intensity and depth in *Tidal Interlude*.

Lahiri brings an extra edge to the lived familiarity in spaces urban; wild; touristy or solitary. Everything is under his curious gaze and ideas and images cartel in bizarre alchemy and gets converted into texts of passionate radiance and density. The poet can convey with all clarity the surge of competing ideas in a masterly way to his intended audiences:

I knew you missed that sailing boat,
All was not well–your eyes told
Renewal, rebirth turning to grimace" (Page 25)

The present collection of his poems unwraps the linguistic and imagistic fairyland where each item — a vigorous gale or a fond twig or a wandering star — is compiled with precision and is a discourse, like each symphony of Beethoven. The poems here come out of the dynamics of the tide, more of life itself. Lahiri reminds us of Sylvia Plath who has also shown a larger truth about how emotional suffering makes people feel isolated under their own airless glass jar. The poet thus writes:

> I script the footprints but missing lines,
> That drags me backward
> And then I know the gentle push
> Of the sheared wallflower." (Page 55)

Lahiri's poems definitely add to the oeuvre of Indian poetry in English.

Title: *Tidal Interlude*
Author: Gopal Lahiri
Page: 70
ISBN: 13: 978-81-931666-7-3
Edition: Paperback, 2015
Published by: Shambhabi–The Third Eye Imprint, India
Price: INR 250 | USD 9.50

Sitayayan : A Review of Nandini Sahu's *Sita*

This book of poetry attempts to deconstruct the epic subject of the female stereotype. Epic is a predominantly masculine form of poetic utterance; the history of literature as well as conventional literary theories would augment that presumption as well. An attempt has been made here to construct a similar exercise on the ancient epic that has in multiple ways ordained Indian systems of thought and gender relations. This text stands as a subversive deconstruction of the epic from the subject position of one subalterned by gender. Traversing a considerable space in literary time (Ramayana age – contemporary time) the author, acclaimed poet and academician Prof. Nandini Sahu chooses inter-semiotic modes for argument. The reviewer's interest in this text primarily stems from the fact of Indianness of theme and the questioning of gender from a contemporary standpoint. The fact of vernacular and English as a medium of thought has further been analyzed in the course of the poem. *Sita* transcends any temporal barriers to the metaphor of *Rama Rajya* and questions subalternity inherent in stereotyping of gender, in a way that has always thwarted the process of evolution of the nation and its 'civil' society.

"Woman must put herself into the text – as into the world and into history – by her movement." (Helene Cixous: *The Laugh of the Medusa*). The urge to revisit these lines written in 1975 originally in French (and made available in English through the translation of Keith and Paula Cohen in 1976) which laid the basic roadmap for what came to be known as 'Ecriture Feminine' came from the very first glance at the 'Preface' to *Sita (A Poem)* by Nandini Sahu. At the very outset, Nandini categorically states that her long poem is not a re-telling of *The Ramayana* in any of its varied extant forms; it is, as she puts it, *"penned as a poetic memoir of the heroine of the epic Sita, told in the first-person narrative"* (Page v) (Italics mine). The poet herself calls it a first-person narrative; wherein she attempts not just a radical displacement of the focus of the long poem from patriarchal/ chauvinistic social ethos, but catapults the text on a universal eco-feminist plane by proclaiming through it the 'Sitaness' of every woman. As she writes:

> Call her what you may – Sita, Janaki,
> Vaidehi, Ramaa – she is Woman
> She is every woman, the propagated,
> interpolated role model. (Page 1)

The twenty-first century Sita, as Nandini writes, is 'truly animated to this living, present living.'

Instead of being a passive adherent to the deification that runs at the sub-textual level as a patriarchal ploy (and is the staple of most parent texts) to hem her consciousness of 'incandescent strength' (Canto XXV), the refrain of Sita as the woman (above and beyond a rarefied soul) being in love with her husband and expecting love in return is very eloquent. Ordinarily, for a woman in the public domain, such a professing of the person would be unexpected, but as a *careful* perusal of the text will show, this is not the same as reverence for *'Maryada Purusottam'* that pervades the epic. Rather it is the mark of Sita's innate womanliness that Nandini designates as her 'Sita-ness.' Thus *Rama Rajya* becomes a chauvinist's utopia even as Sita's narrative is pervasive with her knowledge of these failings on the part of her 'protector,' and thereby the state.

The 'difference' between Sita's/Nandini's ability to see through the fault lines of Rama, much of which may be the domain of masculinity studies, and her conscious choice of defining 'dharma' as the dutiful wife gives a whole new facet to her character. Thus while on the one hand, she mentors herself to comprehend the 'meaning of wifehood' which primarily entails the fourteen years of exile and readies herself as the home-maker in dire straits, she simultaneously soliloquies on the injustice being meted out to Urmila, the docile wife of Lakshman who must now endure more than a *yug* of solitude that is killing, to say the least. The question Sita poses to Rama merits an answer, though there is none:

> Where did your
> unending compassion to values and duty
> vanish in this agenda of pain for her? (Page15)

Sita (A Poem) conjoins upon women the resolute task of summoning courage in the face of the subversive social tag of blasphemy, to stand up for their rights and protest its violation. This explains the demystification of the epic language and the creation of a discourse that easily crisscrosses time and space. In the same vein, the poet must be credited for being free of any undue feminist slant. Sita the champion of women's rights is also her critic when it comes to her obsession for the golden deer which is beyond what is ordained by Mother Nature.

The multi-dimensional vision of Sita with which she creates a female bonding that encompasses 'tales of incredible exoneration and extraction' is indeed praiseworthy. Just as the exiled queen of Ayodhya can look beyond her imminent doom and care for Urmila, so also a Sita liberated from the imprisonment of Ravana after victory to the vanarasena led by Rama cannot but feel for the widowhoods of Mandodari and Sulochana. At one level they are today what she would be in the days to come – victims of boundless male ego:

> Was Sita
> unacceptable to you in her exilic raiment,
> a fount of raw energy that
> she was? The purity-pollution debate –
> had it already started
> in your mind? (Page 68)

Thus the female body becomes the site for contestation between private-public spheres, as the husband who is royalty designate, ensures that denunciation of the woman who lived alone in another man's house without any of her clan to protect her, must happen in the public domain. Within the span of a mere twelve lines, we have Rama saying:

> "She was solely responsible for this war, this disaster." (Page 69)

In this view, it is oppressive and patriarchal conceptual frameworks, and the behaviors that give rise to, that sanction, maintain, and perpetuate the twin dominations of women and nature. Rama criticizes her in public,

> You were born of unknown parenthood
> Thus your purity was already half challenged
> Now you have lost it all; you must not be
> chaste anymore. (Page 70)

If the reader can look upon the text as a plea for gender sensitization, then Rama's protracted castigation of Sita would appear, not as the stripping of this woman who is virtue incarnate, but as a dramatic monologue that only strips the accuser of all vestiges of glory ever attributed to him. Nandini gives us an example of Rama's intellectual and emotional disrobing of Sita who has considered him her destiny and destination. That way, this text stands the test of what Gordimer has privileged as 'inward testimony'. Nandini scripts the "Sitayan," with a deft hand.

Works Cited: Cixous, Helene, Keith Cohen, and Paula Cohen. *The Laugh of the Medusa, Signs*, 1.4 (1976): 875-893

Title: *Sita* (A Poem)
Author: Nandini Sahu
Page: 129
ISBN: 978-93-83888-19-1
Edition: Paperback, 2019
Published by The Poetry Society of India, Gurgaon
Price: INR 220 | USD 20

Teasing Clues of Life: a review of *Resonance*

Indian English poetry is no more a toddler but has reached its heyday of youth. One can hear its resonance from the poets of Odisha. *Resonance: English Poetry from Poets of Odisha*, edited by Chittaranjan Misra, Jaydeep Sarangi, Mona Das ushers in a mood of enchantment, the poets of this Anthology grab attention with their poise and expression. "Indian- English- Poetry" of the volume under review "can be viewed as an ongoing juxtaposition of conflicting ideas related to 'cultural diversity' of the country and 'cultural difference' as a globally accepted marker of identity"(Page 6). In the Introduction to the volume, the editors write: "Poetry from Odisha can be seen as an attempt at a metonymic exposition to Indian English Poetry seed of this idea has resulted in this anthology. Odisha as a state remains fairly low-key not only outside India but also within India. There is no understood Odia identity say in the manner of a Bengali or Punjabi stereotype, which almost defines an Indian due to a lack of any other established identities. In a way, this benefits the Odia poet or to be more accurate, the poet from Odisha, to maintain a neutral gaze and bringing objectivity to their writing"(Page 7).

The sense of location that the Odisha English poets construct is about cultural specificity refracted through poets' sensibility and power of fashioning imagery. Since many of these poets are bilingual poets writing in Odia as well as English their works in both the languages signify a rootedness while opening out to the world. The anthology also adds established and new voices from Odisha and also outside the state and the country. Most of the poets here have been published widely and have earned an international reputation. The editors have gracefully added a few poems in memory of those they have lost.

Bibhu Padhi is one of the most formidably intellectual poets of his generation with stellar achievements. His poems "Night sounds," "And then Darkness," "Trust," straddles a mind-boggling canvas. In "Finding and Losing," he writes: "I'm alone, and the usual doors /of escape are shut and sealed, / as though they were meant / for somebody else's life" (Page 26). Here each word is a world that resonates and leaves a fine aftertaste. "Guitar" of Bipin Patsani reminds one of David Russell playing the guitar live, the poet writes "Are you not a meeting place of voices? / In you I hear the roar of the sea / And the quiet storms above; / In you only, in unlimited space I move/ And meet eternity" (Page 28). Deba Patnaik's "Death is not Dying" tugs a chord in the heart. He explores memory and desire through the lens of loss and despair. The grief is beyond personal, "Who says death is lonely? / Living is" (Page 36). "Memory is a treacherous rainbow-arch / to blind alleys – unending, serpentine. / Memory is a shadow-play tricking us into believing". The approach is to arrive at propositions which locate poetry as an archive for memory. "Winter" of Chittaranjan Mishra bridges the past and present memories. The technique of the movements in the poem is melodious, innovative, and touches the readers with beautiful oscillations of keynotes: "I never thought / This rustle of leaves / Would remind me / Of their absence ... I never thought / This winter/ I would trail/ My wild shadows / On the moonlit shore" (Page 43). "Self" turns out to be a many-layered conversation in which the poet explores an audacious range of virtuosities, his curiosity about various aspects of the self-stirred by intense exchanges, and his understanding of melody, rhythm, and movement of life/lives enhanced by the interface.

Chinmoy Jena in "October" writes about light, shadows, and the simplicity of life. Dilip Mohapatra in "Suffering" writes, "Pain defines and claims its territory / sometimes overtly / sometimes surreptitiously / through pangs of labour ... Suffering is only the / flip side of joy / and bliss / just like the flowers and the thorns / bitter and sweet coexist" (Page 55-56). In suffering, there is no firm figure, nor a clear ground. Suffering remains a nagging thorn in one's life. Durga Prasad Panda in his poem "Today" leaves teasing clues of the role played by media and its aftermath. "Strangely no one was hacked / to death / despite speaking the truth fearlessly. / Today was a perfect day. / Today, the newspapers of the country / were on a day's token strike" (Page 61). Itishri Sarangi dedicates her poem "The Catharsis" to the gang-rape victims, she writes "My innocence is killed, my femininity stripped / Crumbled and trashed / The evil destroyed me" (Page 65). The poem is textured by a smart weave of verbal and physical play. It opens up possibilities of finding a new vocabulary for the mutilated gendered body.

Jayanta Mahapatra has made Cuttack in Odisha (Orissa) a significant place on the national literary scene which dates back to his publication of *Chandrabhaga*. Being the first Indian poet to receive the SahityaAkademi Award for his *Relationship* in 1981 he is an iconic Indian poet. He has received global attention for his inimitable style in the use of English. In "The Road," he speaks of a journey that he undertook to have a handle on some of the unknown dynamics of life. The road however has changed. "It's not the road anymore / along which my mother sent me on errands ... The one I have taken now / appears to fill me with purpose and strength. / But I do not know if it is the happy one" (Page 67). The poet heaves as he stands in front of a monumental gateway of the temple of life, he thinks of 'home.' "Something slithers past as I watch, / from the garden someone left behind in my heart. / I try to think of home. / I come upon tracks of tall pylons in the dust" (Page 67). Jaydeep Sarangi weaves an arboreal yarn around Jhargram with its dense forest and red soil. As one reads the lines the mind is full of tranquillity and calm and is far from the maddening crowd of the suffering city. "I'm from that forest land. / My laurels are made of leaves. / I am fast losing my green leaves / Or only coming to what is really my own. / Jhargram— This is where everything ends in love"(Page 69). "Another day in Kolkata" speaks of the fast-changing demography of Kolkata. "Chances are she'll lose the dream / Settle for fast-growing metro links, high sky rises. / Knight Riders fan the tempo, / The fire of Bangla poems doubles the impact" (Page70). Kumerandra Mallik speaks of sleepwalkers 'looking for the roadside to divinity' (Page 76).

Mamata Dash beautifully pens the life journey of a girl who has travelled alone on a luxury boat waiting to sail the other side in "Alone on a Luxury Boat" (Page 78-79). Mona Dash's concern in "Language" is to dredge out if possible, the 'truth' of 'identity,' a 'truth' manifested in trauma and desire, a truth that baffles the symbolic order of language itself. "We made our changes, we learned our lessons, / our tongues remained the same / foreign words our own" (Page 90). Nandini Sahu in "Who Says Death is the Only Truth" critiques those who wait only for death, and questions whether people can make their own music of life or how capable are they in augmenting the civilization. In "Bridge-In-Making," she writes, "Poetry in English is like a passion for empire building. / It's the subaltern speaking / the words pleading to be universally, intently heard" (Page 99). She reflects upon her past, in the light of which she tries to illuminate the present. A very important *modus operandi* adopted by Sahu, to solve the resistances of her cultural third space is, therefore, to decipher her present predicament of anxiety with the help of her mnemonic reservoir to find a real identity. Namita Rani Panda as a woman gazes back and reclaims the space that is denied to a ravished woman/en to burst the bubble around toxic male hegemony in "The Plead of A Corpse" (Page 107).

Niranjan Mohanty is in search of a stony blueprint that mesmerized the world long ago and is continuing to do so in "The Sun Temple at Konark"(Page 109). Prabhanjan Kumar Mishra also speaks of the wonder called Konark. Pradip Kumar Patra wants to "walk towards the horizon / With the quest of our own" (Page 124). Professor Himansu S. Mohapatra in his essay "Showcasing Odia-English Verse: Pitfalls and Prospects," says, "from Jayanta Mahapatra and Bibhu Padhi to Shanta Acharya and Rabindra K. Swain have paid attention to the diction of their poetry. They have perfected idioms which are supple and resonant" (Page 8). Saroj K Padhi in "Daughter" speaks of how a daughter can with her Midas' touch transform the angst, worries, pain, and suffering into tranquil gold. Swapna Behra in "My Sagacious Dreams" glides nimbly over the frets of life sans any kind of visible effort or scrapping.

Resonance: English Poetry from Poets of Odisha along with its editors looks far beyond geographical boundaries and extends the field of vision to include resonance of life. Hope the researchers, scholars, and readers gain fresh vestiges of poetic perception through the Anthology.

Note: *Chandrabhaga* (2000-) a selection of Indian Writing in English is an online magazine that appears twice a year Summer and Winter. Jayanta Mahapatra is the Editor and Rabindra K. Swain is the managing editor.

Title: *Resonance*
Author: Chittaranjan Misra, Jaydeep Sarangi, Mona Das.
Page: 187
ISBN: 978-93-89615-03-6
Edition: Hardbound, 2019
Published by Authors Press, New Delhi
Price: INR 300

The Celebration of Womanhood:
a review of *Zero Point*

With the release of Nandini Sahu's sixth poetry collection, *Zero Point* (a collection of poems) in New Delhi in August 2018, it is high time we looked at this acclaimed collection of poetry again. Sahu's collection of poems, *Zero Point* is a work deserving of a place amongst classics. While posterity will have the answer for certain, yet in the humble opinion of this reviewer, *Zero Point* will continue to let its lines shine forth for generations to come.

In this collection of poems, each poem is a story in verse. In Sahu's words, "Zero point starts when life comes to a full circle, it's a new beginning-inclusive, compassionate, universal, tolerant, accommodative, acquiescent and patient." Sahu transfuses her intrinsic philosophy into a profoundly spiritual, and gloriously beautiful, experience. Needless to add, she does credit to her Muse. At the same time, Sahu's poetry, belonging to the broad genre of contemporary Indian English Poetry, lends itself to a feminist reading. Her images are drawn from nature, and she often describes daily life, yet, an unmistakable divine spirit, an 'over-soul' is present in the pieces. Consider the poem entitled: "These Days I do Only what the Heart says":

> These evenings I have the time to water the
> Plants without worrying much about the daily
> Homework of my child
> Or about the evening menu.
> I have the rider of leaving the kitchen
> To the cook, the worrying jiffy to time,
> And the wind to blow
> whichever direction it pleases-
> Without my approval.

In the poem "From Dust to Dust: A Voyage," the landscapes and their language are concerned with glocal environmental transitions. In ancient India land was worshipped as a mother, a source of nourishment and plentitude for her children. Man and earth were interrelated by the law of *Rita* which was seen as *dharma,* an ethical goal. Any violation of this respect and integrity between humans and earth would disintegrate the balance in the ecological world. Sahu writes:

> And then the Air went on wandering
> upon blue Water
> Blue was the motif, pure blue,

unguarded and blessed
Why did their guilty tongues stagger
without a purpose?
Was a thirsty yearning woman
denied water amid all
Abundance? Yes water is virtuous in myriad
ways, not evil even
When not good.

The poems in *Zero Point*, as this reviewer strives to show, is of that catalogue; it conjoins upon women the resolute task of summoning courage in the face of the subversive social tag of blasphemy, to stand up for their rights and protest its violation. For her part, Sahu scripts *ecriture feminine* by baring her voice which comes through abject nullification of different versions of, narratives of the woman as a subaltern. Sahu's intervention here becomes pivotal in charting the course of her life and of the text henceforth:

Round the gloom of my lonesome
nightfall ululates a carnival
Of lights,
Like Plato, I trust justice is loftier than injustice,
they
Deliberate it or not! (Page 22).

The poet then unabashedly says,

Swim against the tide.
If anything else, at least
I am a better swimmer!
I have total control of my life
For better or worse.
Unorthodox and unapologetic

Facing life with glee
I swim.
I have become an expert at the game.
I call them colonizers
Who keep me ever dependent
And chum
Who toss me in the tide.
After all the friendly ebb awaits at the end.
("Swimming against the Tide")

The soul, indeed, has its world and exists on its terms. In her works, she has pinpointed the attitudes towards hostility against women grounded in and intertwined with power and sexuality. She has essentially harped on the culturally-specific norms and social relations that have a profound influence on attitudes towards cruelty against the gendered subaltern.

My inner abacus shudders with a truth.
I settle down–
Let the imminent and the moral liberal.
Generations glare at me.
I am irredeemable.
A kind of gender resolution architect.
A perpetual, relentless,
The never-ending impulse towards
the boundaries of the mind and spirit,
Frontiers I lookout as I approach them.
("Living in an Alternative Time")

The last poem in the collection, "The Song of Liberty," is an outstanding work, an apt finale. Here Sahu transcends all temporal barriers and questions subalternity inherent in stereotyping of gender, in a way that has always been a nagging thorn at the heart of the evolution of the Indian nation and its 'civil' society. She also mentions that the subject has been seminal to thoughts across her literary oeuvre, so this means this short poem in a way marks the culmination of Sahu's poetic flair while transcending the ever-fleeting boundaries of the personal and the artistic.

> Yes, I didn't 'have' the vagina.
> A mother and a lover though I had been.
> Until I became
> This vagina-having-vagina-speaking woman.
> Until I re-examined my existence
> With the vagina as a metaphor,
> With an understated brilliance.

It is time now for a confrontation and the final one between the thwarted male ego and the ability of the subaltern to speak. Speak she does, and as is her won't, Sahu collectively questions the commodification of the female body through the paradigms of sin and purity as mind-games.

> But any spiky sharpness won't
> stick into me. Those nights.
> Because there was no none vagina.
> He picked the parts of my body he
> Wanted.
> No lips, no none breasts.
> No neck no nape no none cheeks.
> Just the vagina. The dry-like-fig vagina.

To take a leaf out of her life is to re-define freedom— her rejection of male hegemony that is upheld as an illustration of the highest dignity of a just woman. It must be remembered, this freedom, this liberty has come about only after she has lived out the entire purpose of her life amidst all odds. Such organic criteria of completeness have been her own making, in keeping with Nature's purpose of womanhood; she has neither ever paid any heed to scrupulous voices, nor does she now need to be perturbed by continuing debates over her purity and pollution.

She denies no knowledge, excludes nothing, ventures truth in all its mysterious complexity. The living and the loving spirit of *Nandini* in her assert herself in her verses:

> Let love, humane, though frail, sway
> The coming days
> Of Nandini, in Nandini.
> Beyond Nandini. (Page 43)

Nandini's portrayal of Nandini thus comes to us through a gendered postcolonial adaptation of an allegory (Preface: 9) in a way that interrogates shared concerns over the ever-evolving relationship between a woman and her milieu, simultaneously narrativizing her many selves through ever-renewing discourses.

Title: *Zero Point* (a collection of poems)
Author: Nandini Sahu
Page: 95
ISBN: 978-93-88008-51-0
Edition: Paperback, August 2018
Published by Authors Press, New Delhi
Price: INR 250 | USD 12

Poetic Gallery of Urban Life

Urban Reflections: *Photography and Poetry In Dialogue* is a book dedicated to all street artists and urban dwellers. While we walk in the city many times we are present and at the same time absent closing our eyes to people, to things near. Myriad thoughts cross our mind while we are caught up in matters of everyday life and we walk the street lost in glamorous sights. The foreword to the book says, "this book wants to unravel the beauty and politics of contemporary city space in the Americas. It wishes to create a dialogue between photography, poetry, and street art." Street art is unofficial, independent visual art created usually in public locations for public visibility. Sometimes it takes the form of guerrilla art, which has an intention to make a bold personal statement about the society in general in which the artist lives in.

Dr. Wilfred Raussert is chair of North American and Inter-American Studies at Bielefield University, Germany. He is director of the International Association of Inter-American Studies, author and editor of 20 scholarly books. Dr. Ketaki Datta is an Associate Professor of English in a government college in Kolkata, India. She has two novels, two translated novels, and a book of poems. Thus their practices may have been divergent, but it is the sense of evanescence and mellowness which the rapidly changing American city induces brings them together— an introspective writer like Ketaki Datta so captivated by mortality and Wilfred Raussert, whose photography is marked by dynamism and vigour even as he tries to capture fleeting moments of poignance before they are shattered by harsh realities of urban life.

The book begins with the photograph of the street art of Jim Morrison (photograph paired with its text on the facing page), the American singer, songwriter, and poet, who served as the lead vocalist of the rock band, *The Doors*. Due to his poetic lyrics, his widely recognized voice, unpredictable and erratic performances, the mystery regarding his untimely death he is regarded by music critics and his fans as one of the most iconic and influential frontmen in rock history. Datta writes, "Jim Morrison, after singing such / Fiery numbers, / How could you succumb to/ Nullity, under alien stars?" (Page 1-2). A photograph of a man wearing a 'luchador' mask, fine street art in a canteen prompts Datta to write, "A bizarre logo 'luchador' / Above / Marks the canteen as unique, / The closed eyes of a man / With close-knit thick brows. (Page 3-4). Thus this unique dialogue of poetry with photography of street art becomes an exercise in producing the cultural history of the American people.

The photograph called "Sun-dried Butterflies," bypassed the lure of mythology and steered clear of gender strait-jacketing. "Look, her attire has a thousand flowers / On it, that could easily be exchanged / With the sundry butterflies / Painted on the wall! (Page 4-5). Various photographs of Raussert that speak of distinct street art introduce the theme, delving into enigmatic poetry of Datta that inadvertently, spontaneously merge into strange, unbidden shapes. An interesting photograph of Buddha sitting in the meditating posture in the background with a posh-car and the owner in the foreground, busy in wiping the last speck of dust on the chassis of the car maps Raussert's journey from an artist through conversations with himself. This is matched with Datta's tentative tapestry of ideas, cursory sketches: "With a duster in his hand, / He keeps dusting away / The last speck of dirt, / That might sit firm on it, / but,can no way– / Work is worship to him, / Different God is Buddha! (Page 10-11).

"Cleansing The Countenance," the photograph of artfully weathered street art shows the countenance of a glamorous damsel, with a car in the foreground carrying an advertisement which promises of maintenance/Carpet Cleaning, takes on the immediacy of an unfolding drama. The poet writes, "Cobwebby maze beneath thy face? / Who again would take the risk of / Cleaning the shadowy trail / On thy right cheek?/And who cleaned thy left cheek—come, tell! (Page 14-15). In "A Tale of Walking In and Leaving," beguiling imminence imbues Raussert's landscape, while Datta's poem pulsates with the heave and jostle of threadbare fragments. "Anno Domini begins and / The child stands as a dividing line? Between the Timenascent, / And the Time-going, going, gone!" (Page 17-18). "A Tale of Walking In and Leaving" unveils a fragile mind space where blurred, fluid childhood recall seems to float and coalesce into dark intimations, time stands still.

The photography of "Caught In Between" has a simple anchor of binaries: stillness and movement "a man caught unawares / between two images /Of the same lady on the wall / Throwing avid gazes ... But his pose was normal, sans any air(s) / Though he had no choice in the pair, / As they were mirror-reflected images / Though he would not by mistake be in cages!" writes Datta (Page 25-26). The rootedness of Raussert is matched by the reaching out of Datta, this is unique! "Tricky Thing" shows two street artists spray painting the walls weaving a face out of an off-beat, infectious rhythm. The poet writes, "Representation is a tricky thing / It depends on you and your positioning / Representation believe me means complication / It depends on you and your competition in the ring / To make the representation of representation an / authentic thing" (Page 27-28). "Green In Hue"(Page 29-30) is a kind of private soliloquy while "Secret Sharers" (Page 30-31) traces an insidious montage with silhouetted figures.

"Man and Music" warns against a proprietary, wilful degradation of the murals created affectionately in the walls of the cities of America, "While the roads keep winding and winding / They might jam against oblivion / The mural washed away / Even before tomorrow" (Page 33-34). "Urban Mobilities" speaks of Raussert's wry obeisance to Time's ravages, Datta writes; "The fresh morning air pushes him onward / He looks ahead / Hoping to leave the crossroads behind" (Page 37-38). "In Awe" speaks of the remarkable walls the street artists created are as much about forbidding barriers as about passages of surreptitious communication. The photograph "Come and Dance With me" (Page 41-42) delights the readers in a cosmic dance that soars from notional micro to macro scales. Raussert's photograph of the woman in "Walk to Walk" shows an onlooker curiously self-absorbed in meditative anxiety, while Datta weaves fine lines with ease. "Moves off he, leaving the wall behind, / His misconception, his surging desire / All seemed so blind! / Smiled he again to himself and walked on / How was he befooled, by such impish an emotion?!" (Page 53-54).

Urban Reflections: Photography and Poetry in Dialogue can be thus read, enjoyed, shared, in the public spaces of our cities: cafes, parks, street corners, the metro, the bus. This unique book is a poetic paperback gallery of urban life. It pleases the eyes of the readers, it inspires the mind of the readers, it infectiously touches the reader's soul and helps people to open their eyes to the city spaces around them beyond consumption. It is an asset to the individual, and the library as well!

Title: *Urban Reflections: Photography and Poetry in Dialogue*
Author: Wilfred Raussert & Ketaki Datta
Page: 60
ISBN: 978-3-946-507-31-4
Edition: Paperback,2018
Published by KIPU, Bielefeld University, Germany
Price: USD 30